CATCH A WHALE BY THE TAIL

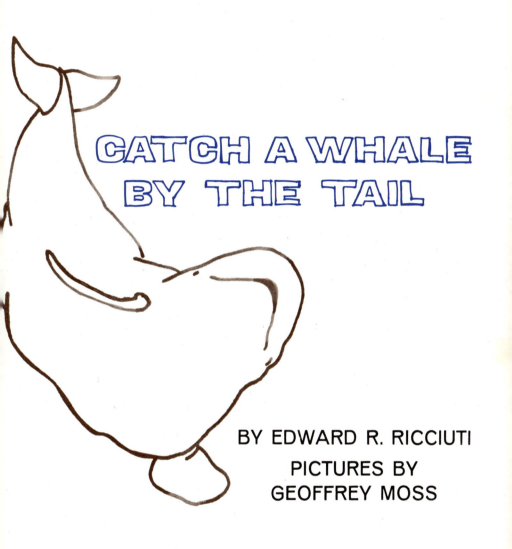

CATCH A WHALE BY THE TAIL

BY EDWARD R. RICCIUTI

PICTURES BY
GEOFFREY MOSS

A Science I CAN READ Book

Harper & Row, Publishers   New York, Evanston, and London

TO CHIQUI, ANNIE, AND TINA

Chapter

1

Robert the white whale
lives at the aquarium.
He swims by himself
in a big tank
full of cold seawater.

7

Sometimes he floats
near the surface.
Sometimes he rolls over
on his back
and flips his tail.

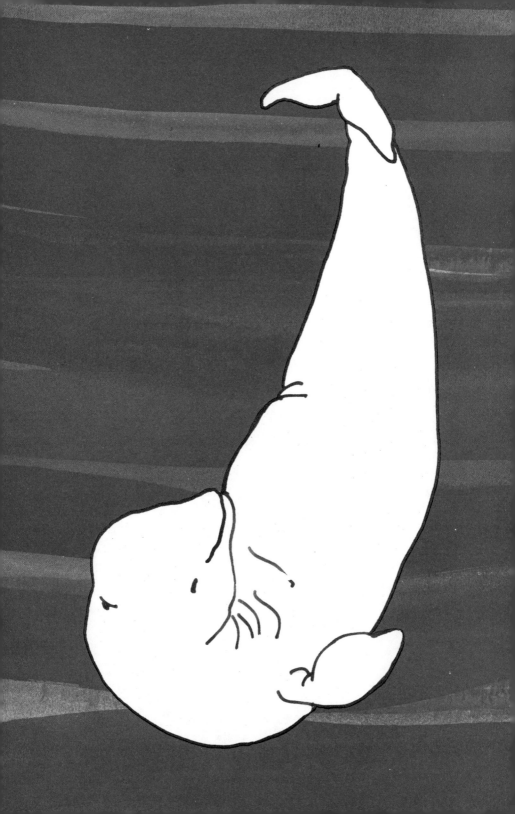

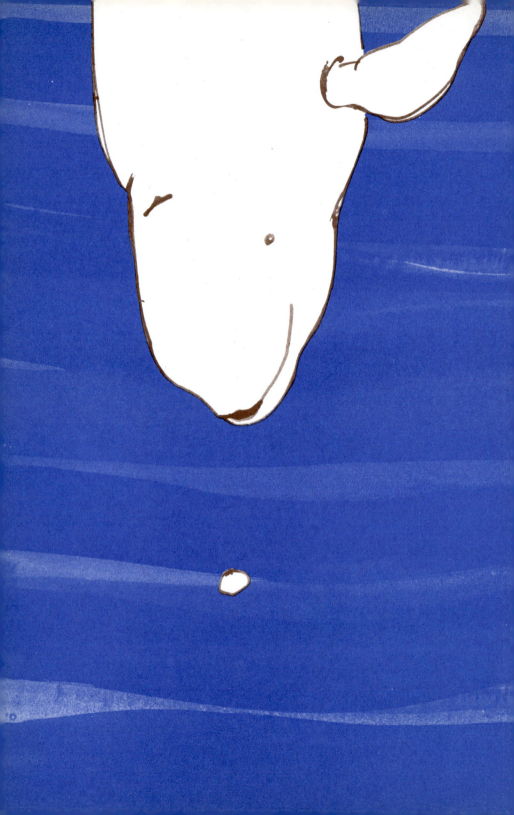

Sometimes Robert plays with a pebble.
He picks up the tiny pebble
with his mouth.
Then he drops it
and slowly follows the pebble
as it sinks.

As he goes down
Robert looks bumpy and saggy
like a giant sweet potato.

But when he comes up for air,
Robert looks like a submarine—
slim and smooth.

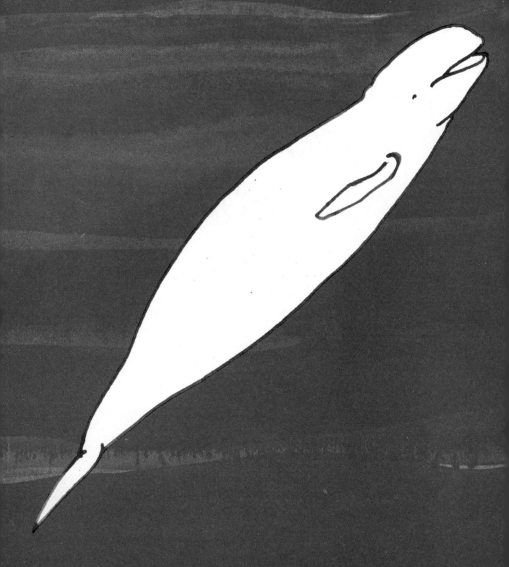

Whales are not fish.

Fish breathe underwater. Whales cannot.

They are mammals.

Mammals must have air to breathe.

Robert breathes through a blowhole

on top of his head.

When he goes underwater,

he closes his blowhole.

He is really holding his breath.

People come to the aquarium

to watch Robert.

Sometimes Robert watches them.

This man is called the aquarium curator.

He takes care of all the animals
at the aquarium.

He likes to see people watch Robert.

His helpers are called the aquarium keepers.

The curator and the keepers
caught Robert in the sea
way up North.

Robert is a white whale.

He is not the biggest
kind of whale.

The biggest whales are the blue whales.

They are bigger than any other animal—

as big as a whole herd of elephants.

The white whale
does not even weigh as much
as one small elephant.

White whales are just right
for the aquarium.

White whales feed on fish and squid.
Sometimes they chase fish up rivers.
People who live in the North
call white whales "sea canaries."
That is because the whales "sing."
They make a lot of noise underwater.
They squeal, hoot, and clack
as they swim.
Scientists want to know
why a whale makes noises.
They come to the aquarium
to listen to Robert.
But Robert hardly ever squeals,
or hoots, or clacks.

"What is wrong with Robert?"

says the curator.

"Maybe he misses the ocean up North."

"But he has a little ocean here,"

says Keeper Pete.

"He has plenty of fish to eat.

He even has people to watch.

Could Robert be lonely?" asks Keeper Pete.

"Maybe you are right!" says the curator.

"We must go up North

to catch a friend for Robert."

Chapter

2

It takes all day
to fly to the North.
That is where the white whales live.
When the curator and keepers get there,
they camp near a river.
This is where the white whales
hunt for fish.
It is summer in the North,
but it is cool here even in summer.

23

The keepers talk and joke
as they set up their tents.
Tomorrow will be a hard day,
but the men do not mind.
The waves roar on the rocky shore.
Seabirds flit over the spray,
snatching up little fish.

In the morning
there is a fine breeze.
Now the men must find the white whales.
The curator uses an airplane.
The pilot shouts: "Down below!"

The curator sees many whales in the sea.

They are headed for the river.

Some are leaping.

Some are diving.

Some are catching fish.

The curator sees big male whales.

They are called bulls.

He sees female whales.

They are called cows.

And he sees a few young whales.

They are called calves.

Calves are dark gray.
They are born the color of a rainy sky.
As they get older and bigger
their color gets lighter and lighter.
By the time they are five years old,
they are white.
The curator wants to catch a whale
that is about five years old.
He wants a female that is
younger than Robert.

The curator and keepers return to camp.
They put on rubber suits
to keep warm in the cold water.
Eskimos and Indians who live here
have come to help catch the whale.
They have brought canoes.

33

"Let's go," shouts the curator.
"Push off!"
Brrrrrmmmmmmm. Motors roar.
Boats whiz through the sea.

The seabirds scatter.
The men laugh
and shout to one another.
Who will be first to catch a white whale?

The men steer their boats
toward the mouth of the river.
They chase the whales
like cowboys herding cattle.
The white whales twist and turn.
They want to get away
from the boats.
But the men chase the whales
into shallow water.
The whales cannot dive there.
It is hard for them to swim away.

The curator sees a whale

splashing in the water.

He jumps out of the boat.

The waves come only to his knees.

The keepers jump from their boats too.

So do the Indians and Eskimos.

The men grab the whale
by its tail.
The whale needs its tail to swim.
If the men hold tight,
the whale cannot get away.
It takes strong muscles to hold a whale.
The men hold on with all their might.
The whale tugs and jerks.
Its skin is very smooth and slippery.
Soon the men are as wet as the whale.
They are glad they wore rubber suits.

The men slide a stretcher
under the whale.
"Lift!" shouts the curator.
It takes eight men to do it.
The whale weighs almost as much

as all of the men.
But the men work together,
and the whale plops into the boat.
The whale is not hurt
because it lands on a soft rubber mat.

The curator looks closely at the whale.

It is a cow.

She is almost all white.

She is the right age for Robert.

"Is she old enough to be a mother?"

asks Keeper Pete.

"Almost," says the curator.

The curator laughs

and pats the new whale on the head.

"What shall we call her?"
he asks the keepers.
"She will live with Robert.
Let's call her Roberta."
"*Snnnooorrrrt. Brrraacccckk,*"
Roberta seems to answer
with noises from her blowhole.

Chapter

3

Roberta rides to the aquarium
in an airplane.
Her crate has a soft rubber mat
on the bottom and sides.
There is a little water in the crate.
Roberta must be kept wet
during the long trip.

The curator pours a bucket of water
over Roberta.
He is careful not to pour water
into her blowhole.
The water must be as cold
as icy seawater.
The curator dumps sacks of ice cubes
into the crate.
The pilot turns off the heat
in the airplane.
The curator shivers.
It is too cold for the men.
But it is just right for Roberta.

After many hours the airplane is home.

Roberta rides on the back of a truck

from the airport to the aquarium.

The keepers work carefully.

They slide a sling under Roberta.

A crane picks her up.

A keeper rides the sling

to keep her safe.

Below is the big whale pool.

Two more keepers wait in the water.
They help Roberta swim off the stretcher.
They take her around
her new home.
Roberta is a little stiff
from the long plane ride.
She looks around.
She swims around the pool by herself.

Roberta only gets halfway
across the pool.
There is a fence in the middle.
Something is on the other side
of the fence.
That something is peeking
through the fence.
That something is Robert.

For a few minutes Robert just watches.

Then he spins around.

He churns the water with his tail.

Is he showing off?

Roberta swims closer to the fence.

So does Robert.

Robert clacks his jaws together.

"Clack, clack, clack."

"Wheeeeeeeeh," goes Roberta.

"Squeeeeeeall," goes Robert.

The scientists rush back to the aquarium.

They gather around.

They wonder what it means.

Whatever it means,

Robert is making plenty of noise.

Soon Robert and Roberta
will get to know each other.
The keepers will take away the fence.
Robert and Roberta will
play together.

Soon there may be a baby whale
in the big tank
at the aquarium.

About White Whales

The white whale, *Delphinapterus leucas,* is also called the beluga. White whales live throughout the Arctic seas. They often come as far south as southern Canada. Sometimes they are even seen off the coasts of the northern United States.

For many years, live white whales have been exhibited at the New York Aquarium. Aquarium expeditions which have gone north to collect belugas have been led by Dr. Carleton Ray, a former curator, and Robert Morris, the present curator of the Aquarium.

We gratefully acknowledge the technical assistance of Mr. Morris in the preparation of this book.